Lynda l

Ma

Xmas '91

International Cooking Collection

Novelty Cakes
& Other Novelty Food

International
Cooking Collection

Novelty Cakes
& Other Novelty Food

Janice Murfitt

CONTENTS

Published exclusively for Cupress (Canada) Ltd
20 Torbay Road, Markham, Ontario L3R 1G6 Canada
by Woodhead-Faulkner (Publishers) Ltd, Simon & Schuster International Group

This edition first published 1988
© Woodhead-Faulkner (Publishers) Ltd 1988
All rights reserved
ISBN 0-920691-78-1
Printed and bound in Italy

INTRODUCTION

Novelty cakes and bakes should not only look appealing and taste delicious, but you should enjoy creating them too; they offer the opportunity to let your own ideas show through.

Children often have ideas to contribute to the finishes—they may prefer a different-colored icing—so encourage their involvement. It is worth every minute spent on making the novelties, just to hear their gasps of delight and excitement and to watch their eyes widen as they recognize clowns, mice, snakes and nursery rhyme characters.

The most popular section will undoubtedly be the novelty cakes. Nearly all are made from a basic cake mixture which is simply baked in a cake, loaf, or jelly roll pan, then cut and decorated to form an exciting boat, wishing well, tractor or automobile—and many more are included to appeal to all age groups.

Savory food is often very plain and uninspiring so it's no wonder children disregard it and look for the sweet alternatives. To encourage them to eat more healthily, a selection of savory novelty ideas has been included. They are fun, nutritious, quick to make and will tempt almost any child just out of sheer curiosity. Try introducing a few of these recipes into your party food or simply at a family meal.

The selection of festive novelties may take more time, but the results are very rewarding. Many of the ideas in this chapter would make ideal gifts for family and friends, who will certainly appreciate them.

NOTES

All spoon measurements are level.

Ovens should be preheated to the temperature specified.

Use U.S. grade large eggs unless otherwise stated.

Marzipan should be rolled out on a surface sprinkled with either sifted powdered sugar or superfine sugar.

To make the cakes easier to cut and shape, bake ahead and store in the freezer, or bake a day or two before required and store in an airtight container.

Basic recipes and icings are marked with an asterisk and given in the reference section (pages 74–79). Increase or decrease the quantities in proportion for the amount required.

Finished cakes, covered in molding icing, marzipan or ready-to-roll icing will store for up to 7 days in a warm, dry place either in a cardboard box or loosely wrapped. Cakes covered in butter icing can be stored in the refrigerator for the same period.

NOVELTY CAKES

WISHING WELL

3-egg quantity Quick Mix
  Cake mixture*
1 quantity Quick Molding
  Icing*
green and red food color
¼ cup Apricot Glaze*

assorted sugar flowers
2 sheets rice paper
5 peppermint candy sticks
strawberry flavored
  liquorice lace
FINISHING TOUCH:
8 inch round cake card

Preparation time:
50 minutes plus
making cake
mixture and icing,
and drying time
Cooking time:
40–45 minutes
Freezing:
Recommended at
end of stage 2

1. Grease and line two 7 inch cake pans.
2. Divide the cake mixture between the two pans and bake in a 325°F oven for 40–45 minutes, until well risen and springy to touch. Cool on a rack.
3. Color three-quarters of the icing pale green and a quarter red.
4. Cut a 3 inch circle from the center of one cake, remove and trim to a 2½ inch circle using a cutter; cut in half for the well supports.
5. Brush all the cake pieces with apricot glaze. Place the whole cake on the cake card, with the ring cake on top.
6. Roll out three-quarters of the green icing on a surface dusted with cornstarch and use to cover the well, easing into the center and around the side. Trim and mark on a brick design. Cover the well supports with the remaining green icing and mark on a brick design. Use the icing scraps to mold a turning handle. Leave to dry.
7. Mold a bucket (see page 78) from red icing. Leave to dry.
8. Secure some sugar flowers onto the well with apricot glaze. Fold both sheets of rice paper together in half for the roof and stick some flowers around the edge.
9. Carefully cut a hole through the center of each well support using a small cutter or an apple corer. Secure the supports to the well with apricot glaze.
10. Push a peppermint candy stick through the holes in the well supports and wind the strawberry liquorice lace around it; attach the bucket underneath. Attach the turning handle to one end of the stick.
11. Cut 2 holes in the top of each well support and push in the peppermint candy sticks. Place the roof in position.

Illustrated bottom
right: Jewelry Box
(page 8)

JEWELRY BOX

3 tablespoons chocolate
    chips
2-egg quantity Quick Mix
    Cake mixture*
1/4 cup Apricot Glaze*
1/2 quantity Quick Molding
    Icing*

peach food color
silver balls
small candy
FINISHING TOUCH:
7 × 4 inch cake card

Preparation time:
40 minutes plus
making cake
mixture and icing,
and drying time
Cooking time:
35–40 minutes
Freezing:
Recommended at
end of stage 2

Illustrated on
page 7

1. Grease and line a 6½ × 3¾ × 3 inch loaf pan.
2. Stir the chocolate chips into the cake mixture. Place the mixture in the pan and bake in a 325° oven for 35–40 minutes, until well risen and springy to touch. Cool on a rack.
3. Cut a ½ inch slice off the top of the cake for the top. Cut a 1 inch strip off one long side of this lid.
4. Brush all the cake pieces with apricot glaze. Place the cake on the cake card.
5. Color the icing pale peach. Roll out half on a surface dusted with cornstarch and place over the cake. Trim to fit and mark a quilted pattern with the back of a knife.
6. Cover the top and support strip with peach icing. Mark a quilt on the top and press in silver balls. Leave to dry.
7. Roll out a piece of icing into a strip ¼ inch thick. Frill the edge by rolling a cocktail stick back and forth along one side. Place around the top edge of the box.
8. Shape necklaces, earrings and rings from the leftover icing (see page 78), adding small candy and balls for gems. Leave to dry.
9. Place the support along the middle of the box, then place the lid and jewelry in position.

CUCKOO CLOCK

3-egg quantity peppermint
    Quick Mix Cake
    mixture*
1 quantity Butter Icing*
4 teaspoons cocoa powder
orange food color

2 tablespoons Apricot
    Glaze*
8 oz package ready-made
    white marzipan
1/2 ice cream wafer, halved
FINISHING TOUCH:
14 × 9 inch cake card

Preparation time:
40 minutes plus
making cake
mixture and icing
Cooking time:
35–40 minutes
Freezing:
Recommended at
end of stage 2

1. Grease and line an 11 × 7 inch cake pan, 1½ inches deep.
2. Place the cake mixture in the pan and bake in a 325°F

oven for 35–40 minutes, until well risen and springy to touch. Cool on a rack.

3. Divide the butter icing in half. Add 3 teaspoons cocoa, blended with 1 tablespoon boiling water, to one half and orange color to the other half. Beat both thoroughly.

4. Cut and assemble the cake according to Figs i and ii, brushing all the pieces with apricot glaze.

5. Spread the roof, outside of the clock and straight pendulum with chocolate icing, smoothing with a palette knife dipped in hot water. Spread the clock face and round pendulum with orange icing. Assemble on the cake card.

6. Color half of the marzipan orange and roll out on a sugared surface. Cut out 2 circles, using a 5½ inch saucer and a 1½ inch plain cutter. Place in position on the clock face and pendulum. Use the remaining orange marzipan to trim the brown edges of the clock.

7. Color the other half of the marzipan brown, using the remaining cocoa. Roll out thinly and cut out hands, numbers, and strips to trim the orange edges of the clock.

8. Use the brown marzipan trimmings to cover the wafer to represent shutters, and to mold a cuckoo (see page 78). Place the marzipan pieces in position, with the hands pointing to the child's age.

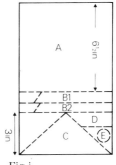

Fig i

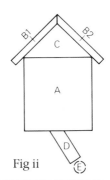

Fig ii

FLOWER BASKET

This pretty basket cake is suitable for almost any age or celebration.

3-egg quantity lemon Quick Mix Cake mixture*

1 quantity Quick Molding Icing*

pink and lavender food color

2 tablespoons Apricot Glaze*

FINISHING TOUCHES: 7 inch fluted round cake card

foil

3 yards of ¹/₂ inch wide pink ribbon

Preparation time: 50 minutes plus making cake mixture and icing, and drying time

Cooking time: About 1 hour

Freezing: Recommended at end of stage 2

1. Grease and line the base of a 7 inch fluted brioche pan.

2. Turn the cake mixture into the pan and make a deep depression in the center. Bake in a 325°F oven for 1 hour, or until well risen and springy to touch. Cool on a rack.

3. Set aside one-third of the molding icing. Color the rest pale pink.

4. With the cake upside down, brush the base and side with apricot glaze. Roll out the pink icing on a surface sprinkled with cornstarch to a circle large enough to cover the base and side. Lift over the cake and gently press into the flutes. Trim the excess icing from around the fluted edge and reserve, then invert the cake onto the cake card. Brush the top with glaze.

5. Roll out a piece of pink icing into a strip measuring 1 × 4 inches. Cut in half lengthways to make 2 strips.

6. Place one strip on a work surface sprinkled with cornstarch. Using the handle of a fine paintbrush, firmly roll backwards and forwards until the edge of the icing is very thin and begins to frill.

7. Position around half of the top edge of the basket. Repeat with the other pink strip. Make a white frill in the same way from some of the reserved icing and position inside the pink frill.

8. Color half of the reserved icing lavender.

9. Make pink, lavender and white frills as above, using strips only 2 inches long. Roll up the frills to form about 20 flowers, cutting off the stems; roll up white and pink frills together and white and lavender frills together to make some double flowers. Leave to dry.

10. Make a 10 inch long handle from several thicknesses of foil. Wind the ribbon around the foil to cover evenly. Tie

a bow out of the remaining ribbon and fix onto the handle.
Bend the handle and press into the top of the cake.
11. Arrange the flowers on top of the basket.

MERRY-GO-ROUND

Instead of pressed sugar animals, which are not meant to be eaten, use bought animal-shaped cookies.

*3-egg quantity lemon
   Quick Mix Cake
   mixture**
1/2 cup sugar
blue and yellow food color
*1 quantity Quick Molding
   Icing**

*3 tablespoons Apricot
   Glaze**
8 peppermint candy sticks
FINISHING TOUCHES:
*9 inch round fluted cake
   card*
7 inch round cake card

Preparation time:
50 minutes plus
making cake
mixture and icing,
and drying time
Cooking time:
30–40 minutes
Freezing:
Recommended at
end of stage 3

1. Grease and line two 8 inch cake pans.
2. Place two-thirds of the cake mixture in one pan and one-third in the other.
3. Bake in a 325°F oven for 30–40 minutes, until well risen and springy to touch. Cool on a rack.
4. Divide the sugar in half and color blue and yellow. Stir in a few drops of water to make a sandy consistency. Press into animal molds, or shape using cookie cutters on a lined baking sheet. Remove the molds or cutters and leave to set.
5. Color half of the icing blue and half yellow.
6. Place the deeper cake on the fluted cake card and the small cake on the plain cake card. Brush both with apricot glaze. Mark the top of each cake into 8 segments.
7. Roll out the blue icing on a surface dusted with corn-starch and cut out a 9 inch circle. Mark into 8 sections and cut carefully. Position 4 sections of blue icing on alternate segments of each cake, smoothing over the side with your hand and trimming at base. Repeat with the yellow icing.
8. Knead and re-roll the icings separately. Cut out 2 blue and 2 yellow 2¾ inch fluted circles using a cookie cutter. Cut each circle in half. Cut 2 small fluted circles for the top and mold a tiny cone shape.
9. Place the smaller cake on a bowl, then stick the semi-circles onto the side of the cake with apricot glaze, matching the colors, to form a scalloped edge. Position the small fluted circles and cone in the center, securing with apricot glaze.
10. Press the candy sticks into the base cake 1½ inches in from the edge, at equal intervals. Leave to dry.
11. Place the sugar shapes by the candy sticks. Carefully place the small cake on top of the candy sticks.

JILL OR JACK IN THE BOX

This cake will delight any child. For Jack, make the top of the box, the body and hat blue. Color the hair brown and mold it in a short style. If marzipan is not a favorite, replace it with 1 quantity of Quick Molding Icing*.

3 tablespoons chocolate chips

*3-egg quantity Quick Mix Cake mixture**

1 lb ready-made white marzipan

pink, blue and yellow food color

*3 tablespoons Apricot Glaze**

2 oz alphabet candies

FINISHING TOUCH: 6 inch square cake card

Preparation time: 50 minutes plus making cake mixture
Cooking time: 20–25 minutes
Freezing: Recommended at end of stage 3

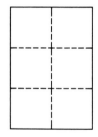

Fig i

1. Grease and line a 13 × 9 inch jelly roll pan.
2. Stir the chocolate chips into the cake mixture, then place in the pan.
3. Bake in a 325°F oven for 20–25 minutes, until well risen and springy to touch. Cool in the pan, then turn out and remove the paper.
4. Set aside 2 oz of the marzipan. Cut the rest in half and color one portion pink and the other blue.
5. Cut the cake according to Fig i and stack 4 pieces on top of each other using apricot glaze, to make the box.
6. Roll out the pink marzipan thinly on a sugared surface and cut out 3 pink squares, to fit 2 opposite sides and the top of the box. Knead the trimmings together.
7. Roll out the blue marzipan and cut out 2 blue squares to fit the 2 remaining sides of the box; place on the cake card. Knead the trimmings.
8. Take one of the remaining pieces of cake and cover the top with pink marzipan and the bottom with blue marzipan. Trim the edges with pink and blue strips of marzipan to make the lid. Knead the trimmings.
9. Cut the remaining piece of cake into 2 circles, using 2 inch and 1½ inch plain cutters.
10. Color the remaining pink and blue marzipan each a shade deeper.
11. Divide the reserved white marzipan in half; color one piece yellow.
12. Brush the cake circles with apricot glaze and cover the larger piece with the deep pink marzipan. Press loosely over and trim roughly. Place in the center of the box. Make a frill with deep blue marzipan and place on top of the body.

13. Mold white marzipan around the small cake circle and place in position on the frill, for the head.

14. Make hair from yellow marzipan, and features, ribbons and a hat from blue and pink marzipan. Press in position.

15. Position the lid at the back of the box, leaning against Jill. Using apricot glaze, press colored candies into the sides of the box.

WINDMILL

*3-egg quantity orange
    Quick Mix Cake
    mixture**
*1½ quantities Quick
    Molding Icing**
*blue, red, brown and
    yellow food color*

*3 tablespoons Apricot
    Glaze**
*2 tablespoons flaked
    coconut*
2 ice cream wafers
FINISHING TOUCH:
*8 inch fluted round cake
    card*

Preparation time:
45 minutes plus
making cake
mixture and icing,
and drying time
Cooking time:
50–55 minutes
Freezing:
Recommended at
end of stage 3

1. Grease and line the bases of 3 pudding bowls with the following capacities: 2 pints, 1 pint, and ½ pint.
2. Place 2 teaspoons of the cake mixture in a paper cake case. Half-fill the bowls with the remaining mixture.
3. Bake in a 325°F oven for 15–20 minutes for the paper case, 30–35 minutes for the small, 40–45 minutes for the medium-size, and 50–55 minutes for the large cake, until well risen and springy to touch. Cool on a rack.
4. Color three-quarters of the icing pale blue. Divide the remaining icing into 2 pieces and color red and brown.
5. Brush the cakes with apricot glaze and stack upside down, largest to smallest at the top, to form a windmill shape.
6. Roll out the blue icing on a surface dusted with cornstarch, to a shape wider at the base and tapering towards the top, and carefully wrap around the windmill to cover completely. Trim to fit and smooth with hands dusted with cornstarch. Place on the cake card, with the join at the back. Leave to dry.
7. Mold a doorstep and a small dome from a little of the icing trimmings. Color the remaining trimmings darker blue, roll out and cut out 2 door and 10 window shapes. Trim the edges with red icing. Position on the windmill, securing with apricot glaze.
8. Color the coconut yellow. Brush the cake card with apricot glaze and sprinkle with the coconut.
9. Cut the wafers in half diagonally and brush with apricot glaze on one side. Roll out the remaining dark blue icing very thinly and use to cover the wafers. Attach the wafer sails to the windmill with icing trimmings, then position a small dome of red icing in the center of the sails.
10. Mold 1 pair of clogs from red icing, and 2 grain sacks from brown icing; mold a few flowers from any remaining icing (see page 78) and arrange on the board.

GINGERBREAD HOUSE

3-egg quantity
    Gingerbread Dough*
1 quantity Royal Icing*
powdered sugar to sprinkle
¹/₄ lb banana chips
¹/₄ lb jelly beans or
    gumdrops

¹/₄ lb square candies
2 oz chocolate- and
    yogurt-coated raisins
FINISHING TOUCH:
11 inch square cake board

Preparation time:
45 minutes plus
making dough and
icing, and setting
time
Cooking time:
About 10 minutes
Freezing:
Not recommended

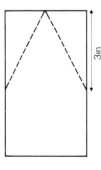

Fig i

1. Roll out a quarter of the dough at a time to an ¹/₈ inch thickness and place each piece on a well-floured baking sheet. Cut the house and garden shapes, following the shaping instructions below, then shape the front and back walls according to Fig. i.
2. Cut out 2 tree shapes using a Christmas tree cutter.
3. Mark lines on the shutters. Angle the side of the chimney. Press the fence posts onto the rails. Shape half a fence piece for the gate. Shape 1 seat and 1 seesaw with support.
4. Bake in a 350°F oven for about 10 minutes. Cool on a rack.
5. Spread the edges of the side and front and back walls with icing and join together to form a box. Place carefully on a cake board.
6. Spread the top edges and the edges where the roof will join with icing and carefully place the roof in position. Hold for a minute to secure, then leave for 30 minutes.
7. Attach the doors at each end, shutters on the front and side walls, and chimney on the roof, securing with icing. Sprinkle the board with powdered sugar to represent snow.
8. Stick the fence and gate around the edge of the board, then place the path, trees, seat and seesaw in position.
9. Tile the roof with banana chips, starting at the edge and working up to the top, securing with a little icing.
10. Decorate the house with candies and raisins, securing with icing. Sprinkle with a little more powdered sugar.

SHAPING INSTRUCTIONS

Two 8 × 6 inch roof shapes
Two 6 × 4 inch side walls
Two 7 × 4 inch front and back walls
Six 1½ × 1 inch window shutters
Two 2 × 1½ inch doors
Five 3 × 1 inch strips for path, seat, seesaw and chimney
Eight 5 × ¼ inch fence rails
Thirty-two 1½ × ¼ inch fence posts.

CAMILLA CATERPILLAR

*2-egg quantity chocolate
    Quick Mix Cake
    mixture**
¼ cup Apricot Glaze*
*1 quantity Quick Molding
    Icing**
*green, red and blue food
    color*

*1 oz colored chocolate
    candies*
2 candy cigarettes
*FINISHING TOUCH
    (optional):*
10 inch square cake board

Preparation time:
30 minutes plus
making cake
mixture and icing,
and drying time
Cooking time:
20–25 minutes
Freezing:
Recommended at
end of stage 1

Illustrated on
page 23

1. Divide the cake mixture between 18 greased muffin cups and bake in a 325°F oven for 20–25 minutes, until well risen and springy to touch. Cool on a rack.
2. Sandwich the cakes, tops together, in pairs with apricot glaze. Press each pair gently into a round shape, then brush all over with apricot glaze.
3. Color three-quarters of the icing pale green. Divide into 9 pieces. Roll out each piece on a surface dusted with cornstarch to a circle large enough to cover one pair of cakes. Trim the icing to fit and smooth with hands dusted with cornstarch.
4. Arrange on a cake board or other surface in an 'S' shape. Secure the chocolate candies along the top. Press the candy cigarettes into one end for antennae and press a small ball of green icing onto each antenna.
5. Divide remaining icing into three and color blue, red, and pink with a few drops of food color. Cut out a 1½ inch pink circle using a plain cutter; attach to the head end with apricot glaze, to resemble a face.
6. Make a mouth, eyes, nose and a hat from the red and blue icing. Press into position and leave the icing to dry.

SNOOKER TABLE

*3-egg quantity coffee
    Quick Mix Cake
    mixture**
*¾ lb ready-made white
    marzipan*
*green, brown, pink, blue,
    black, yellow and red
    food color*

*3 tablespoons Apricot
    Glaze**
FINISHING TOUCHES:
12 × 7 inch cake card
edible black food color pen

1. Grease and line an 11 × 7 inch rectangle cake pan, 1½ inches deep.

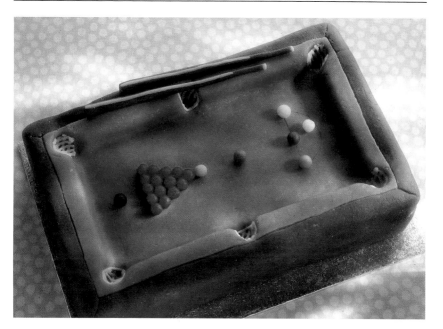

2. Place the cake mixture in the pan and bake in a 325°F oven for 35–40 minutes, until well risen and springy to touch. Cool on a rack.

3. Set aside a quarter of the marzipan. Cut the rest in half and color one portion green and the other brown.

4. Cut a 1 inch wide strip off one long and one short edge of the cake. Cut the strips in half lengthways. Brush the cake and strips with apricot glaze, then trim and fit the strips around the top edge of the cake to make a raised edge. Place on the cake card.

5. Roll out the brown marzipan thinly to a piece long enough to wrap around the sides of the cake and wide enough to overlap half of the top rim. Trim to fit.

6. Roll out the green marzipan thinly; use to cover the top of the table and join the brown marzipan. Smooth the top.

7. Using a ½ inch plain cutter or end of an icing tip, cut out the 6 pockets around the table. Roll out thin lengths of white marzipan, using a flat hand, and trim to make 6 lattice squares to fit the pockets. Shape a ball and 2 cues from brown marzipan; trim cues with white marzipan. Shape a ball from the remaining green marzipan.

8. Mold 5 balls from the white marzipan and color pink, blue, black and yellow; leave one white.

9. Color the remaining marzipan red and shape 15 balls. Leave the balls to dry. Mark the table with the food color pen, then place the cues and balls in position.

Preparation time:
45 minutes plus making cake mixture
Cooking time:
35–40 minutes
Freezing:
Recommended at end of stage 2

TOADSTOOL HOUSE

4-egg quantity Quick Mix
    Cake mixture*
1 quantity Quick Molding
    Icing*
red, green and yellow food
    color

3 tablespoons Apricot
    Glaze*
3 tablespoons flaked
    coconut
2 brandy snaps
FINISHING TOUCH:
    8 inch round cake board

Preparation time:
45 minutes plus
making cake
mixture and icing,
and drying time
Cooking time:
55–60 minutes
Freezing:
Recommended at
end of stage 2

1. Grease and line a 7 inch square cake pan, and grease and line the base of a 1½ quart pudding bowl.
2. Place one-third of the cake mixture in the pan, and two-thirds in the bowl. Bake in a 325°F oven for 25–30 minutes for the square cake and 55–60 minutes for the pudding bowl cake, until well risen and springy to touch. Cool on a rack.
3. Color one-third of the molding icing red.
4. Brush the pudding bowl cake with apricot glaze. Roll out the red icing on a surface sprinkled with cornstarch to a circle large enough to cover the cake. Carefully place over the dome of the cake and smooth with hands dusted with cornstarch. Trim off the excess icing underneath and knead the trimmings. Leave the icing to dry on a plate dusted with cornstarch.
5. Cut the square cake into 4 circles with a 3 inch plain cutter and sandwich together with apricot glaze. Roll out half of the white icing to a rectangle, long and wide enough to wrap around the cake like a cylinder. Trim to fit and smooth with hands dusted with cornstarch. Leave to dry.
6. Roll out a little white icing and cut out about twenty-five ½ inch circles with a plain meringue tip. Stick all over the red cake, using a little apricot glaze.
7. Shape 2 red chimneys and white pots. Leave to dry.
8. Set aside a piece of white icing. Cut the rest in half and color yellow and green. Roll out the green icing and cut out a door, doorsteps, and 2 windows. Trim each with a thin piece of red icing. Mold a few flowers from red, yellow and white icing (see pages 78–79).
9. Place the white cake on a board, brush the top with apricot glaze and position the red cake on top. Arrange the chimneys and pots, door and windows.
10. Brush the board with apricot glaze. Color the coconut green and sprinkle on the board. Arrange the flowers around the house. Color the green trimmings darker and press out to resemble foliage: attach to the brandy snaps to represent trees. Secure in position with green icing.

Illustrated bottom:
Camilla Caterpillar
(page 20)

TRAINING SHOES

*3-egg quantity Beaten
    Sponge Cake mixture**
*¹/₄ cup Apricot Glaze**
*1 quantity Quick Molding
    Icing**

*³/₄ lb ready-made white
    marzipan
pink food color
FINISHING TOUCH:
    8 inch square cake card
    (optional)*

Preparation time:
45 minutes plus
making sponge cake
mixture and icing,
and drying time
Cooking time:
15–20 minutes
Freezing:
Recommended at
end of stage 3

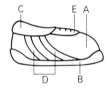

1. Grease and line a 13 × 9 inch jelly roll pan.
2. Place the sponge cake mixture in the pan and bake in a 350°F oven for 15–20 minutes, until well risen and springy to touch.
3. Turn out onto sugared · paper, trim the edges, and spread with apricot glaze. Roll up firmly from one long edge. Cool on a rack.
4. Color the icing and marzipan pale pink.
5. Cut the jelly roll in half and brush all over with apricot glaze. Roll out half of the pink icing on a surface dusted with cornstarch and use to cover one roll, pressing into position and rounding one end to form a toe shape (A). Repeat with the other roll. Knead the trimmings together.
6. Remove a third of the marzipan, cut in half and roll one piece out to an 8 inch rectangle. Shape into a sole, with a toe and heel end. Place the roll on the sole and press the marzipan into shape (B). Repeat with the other roll and marzipan. Place on the cake card if using.
7. Mold some of the remaining marzipan into 2 horseshoe shapes to fit around the ankle part of each shoe and press in position (C). Mold strips to trim the sides of the shoes (D) and attach. Cut out 2 marzipan 'tongues' (E) and place on top.
8. Using your finger tips, roll out thin pieces of icing to make the laces and bows and place in position. Leave to dry.

HOCKEY STICK

*2-egg quantity Beaten
    Sponge Cake mixture**
*¹/₄ cup Apricot Glaze**
*¹/₂ quantity Quick Molding
    Icing**

*brown, blue, black, yellow
    and green food color
3 tablespoons flaked
    coconut
FINISHING TOUCH:
    10 × 6 inch cake card*

1. Grease and line a 13 × 9 inch jelly roll pan.

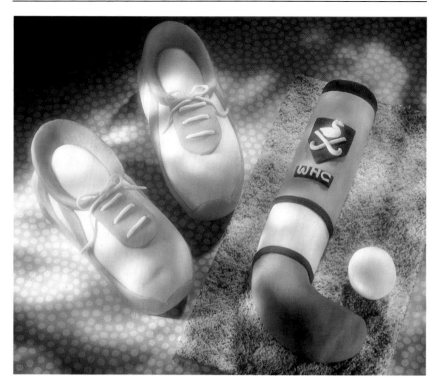

2. Place the sponge cake mixture in the pan and bake in a 350°F oven for 8–10 minutes, until well risen and springy to touch.

3. Turn out onto sugared paper, trim the edges and spread with apricot glaze. Roll up from one long edge and gently curl round one end to form a hockey stick shape. Cool on a rack.

4. Color a quarter of the icing brown, a quarter blue, a little black and a tiny piece yellow; leave the rest white.

5. Roll out the brown icing on a surface dusted with cornstarch and use to cover the curved end of the stick. Cover the next section of the stick with white icing and the remaining part blue. Trim and press into shape.

6. Trim the icing joints with thin strips of black icing and smooth a rounded piece at the end of the handle.

7. Use yellow, blue and black icing to make your own club emblem and initials and place in position on the stick.

8. Mold a ball from the white icing and leave to dry.

9. Brush board with apricot glaze. Color coconut green and sprinkle on the board. Put the ball next to the stick.

Preparation time:
35 minutes plus making sponge cake mixture and icing, and drying time
Cooking time:
8–10 minutes
Freezing:
Recommended at end of stage 3

TELE TOM

3-egg quantity chocolate Quick Mix Cake mixture	*2 tablespoons Apricot Glaze**
*1 quantity Quick Molding Icing**	*FINISHING TOUCHES:*
yellow food color	*10 inch square cake card*
	edible black food color pen

Preparation time:
40 minutes plus making cake mixture and icing, and drying time
Cooking time:
35–40 minutes
Freezing:
Recommended at end of stage 2

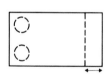

Fig i

2in

Illustrated top right: Birthday Butterfly (page 28)

1. Grease and line an 11 × 7 inch cake pan, 1½ inches deep.
2. Place the cake mixture in the pan and bake in a 325°F oven for 35–40 minutes, until well risen and springy to touch. Cool on a rack.
3. Set aside one-eighth of the icing. Color the rest yellow.
4. Cut a 2 inch strip off one short end of the cake (Fig. i). Place the remaining cake on the cake card and cut out 2 circles using a 2 inch plain cutter. Split the circles in half horizontally to make four, then replace two back in the cake.
5. Trim the strip to a receiver shape.
6. Brush all the cake pieces with apricot glaze.
7. Roll out two-thirds of the yellow icing on a surface dusted with cornstarch to a rectangle large enough to cover the cake. Place over the cake, trim to fit and smooth with hands dusted with cornstarch, pressing the icing slightly into the cut-out shapes.
8. Knead the trimmings together and roll out with the remaining yellow icing. Use to cover the receiver handle; trim and smooth well.
9. Cover the round cake pieces with the remaining yellow icing and fit to the receiver, securing with apricot glaze. Leave to dry.
10. Using a flat hand, roll out a thin piece of yellow icing until about 8 inches long and coil loosely around a pencil covered with cornstarch. Leave until almost set, then carefully remove the pencil.
11. Roll out the reserved white icing and cut out twelve ¾ inch squares and the letters for the person's name, using alphabet cutters or templates.
12. Place the squares in position for digits, securing with apricot glaze. Write on the numbers with the food color pen.
13. Place the receiver in position and attach the coil and letters with apricot glaze.

LADYBUG FAMILY

*2-egg quantity chocolate
    Quick Mix Cake
    mixture**
1 quantity Butter Icing*
red and green food color
*1 tablespoon Apricot
    Glaze**

*3 tablespoons flaked
    coconut*
3 long pieces of liquorice
FINISHING TOUCH:
10 inch round cake board

Preparation time:
30 minutes plus
making cake
mixture and icing
Cooking time:
50 minutes
Freezing:
Recommended at
end of stage 3

1. Grease and line the base of a 1½ quart pudding bowl.
2. Place three-quarters of the cake mixture in the pudding bowl and the rest in 3 paper cake cases.
3. Bake in a 325°F oven for 20 minutes for the small cakes and 50 minutes for the pudding bowl cake, until well risen and springy to touch. Leave to cool, then turn out.
4. Color the icing red and use to cover the cakes, using a palette knife dipped in hot water.
5. Brush the cake board with apricot glaze. Color the coconut green, then sprinkle onto the board.
6. Arrange the ladybugs on the board. Place a strip of liquorice over the center of each ladybug.
7. Wind most of the liquorice, making 2 small coils and one larger. Cut the coils in half to make semi-circles and press in position for the ladybugs' noses.
8. Cut the remaining liquorice into thin slices and arrange as dots over each ladybug.

BIRTHDAY BUTTERFLY

Preparation time:
30 minutes plus
making cake
mixture and icing
Cooking time:
35–40 minutes
Freezing:
Recommended at
end of stage 2

Simple but effective. Choose any small colored candies to decorate the wings, or pipe with colored icing.

*2-egg quantity Quick Mix
    Cake mixture**
1 quantity Butter Icing*
pink food color
*2 tablespoons Apricot
    Glaze**
red decorating gel

1 piece red liquorice
*2 oz red and white jelly
    beans*
FINISHING TOUCH:
10 inch square cake card

1. Grease and line an 8 inch round cake pan.
2. Place the cake mixture in the pan and bake in a 325°F oven for 35–40 minutes, until well risen and springy to touch. Cool on a rack.
3. Color the butter icing pale pink.

Illustrated on page
27

4. Cut the cake in half vertically. Make a scalloped pattern along both cut edges using a 2 inch plain cutter (Fig. i). Arrange 5 of the cut-out pieces between the 2 'wings' to make a body, head and tail (Fig ii).

5. Brush all the pieces of cake with the apricot glaze and leave to set for about 10 minutes.

6. Spread each wing shape carefully with pink butter icing, using a palette knife dipped in hot water. Place on the cake card.

7. Cover the head, tail and body pieces with pink butter icing and place carefully in position.

8. Using the red decorating gel, pipe the outline of the wings, body, head and tail.

9. Use the red liquorice to make 2 antennae. Outline the wings with the jelly beans.

Fig i

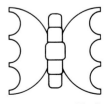

Fig ii

TRACTOR

3-egg quantity Quick Mix Cake mixture*	2 long pieces of liquorice
1 quantity Butter Icing*	5 jelly beans or other candy
blue food color	4 gumdrops
1 mini chocolate roll	1 liquorice twist
4 big oatmeal cookies	bran cereal
2 yogurt cream filled cookies	FINISHING TOUCHES:
4 small candies	8 inch square cake board
15 liquorice sandwich candies	rice paper
	edible black food color pen

Preparation time:
40 minutes plus making cake mixture and icing
Cooking time:
50–55 minutes
Freezing:
Recommended at end of stage 2

Fig i

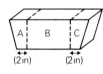

(2 in)   (2 in)

Fig ii

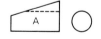

Fig iii

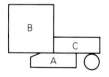

1. Grease and line a 6½ × 3¾ × 3 inch loaf pan.
2. Place the cake mixture in the pan and bake in a 325°F oven for 50–55 minutes, until well risen and springy to touch. Cool on a rack.
3. Color the butter icing blue.
4. Cut a 2 inch slice off each end of the cake (Fig. i). Place piece A cut side down, and trim to the same height as the chocolate roll (Fig ii). Spread with the icing, using a palette knife dipped in hot water, and place with the roll on a cake board.
5. Trim piece C to a rectangle. Spread cake pieces B and C with icing. Turn piece B on its side and position on piece A, with the cut sides becoming the sides of the tractor cab. Balance piece C, cut side down, on piece A and the chocolate roll (Fig iii).
6. Stick the oatmeal cookies together with icing to form 2 thick wheels. Spread the wheels with icing. Attach liquorice around the wheels for tires.
7. Repeat with the smaller cookies.
8. Place the wheels in position and press a candy in the center of each.
9. Cut the liquorice sandwich candies each into 3 slices and arrange in window shapes on the sides, front and back of the tractor cab.
10. Trim the front and back with liquorice strips. Make a radiator grill out of jelly beans or other candy. Position the gumdrops for front and back lights and the liquorice twist for a smoke funnel.
11. Sprinkle the bran cereal over the board to represent a ploughed field.
12. Make 2 personalized license plates using rice paper and the food color pen and attach to the tractor.

TOOT-TOOT ENGINE

3-egg quantity Beaten
   Sponge Cake mixture*
1/3 cup Apricot Glaze*
1 quantity Quick Molding
   Icing*
red food color
3 mini chocolate rolls
5 liquorice sticks
8 long liquorice pieces

6 chocolate buttons
FINISHING TOUCHES:
two 7 × 4 inch cake cards
banana chips
crystallized papaya and
   pineapple
yogurt- and
   chocolate-coated
   raisins

Preparation time:
45 minutes plus
making sponge
cake mixture and
icing, and drying
time
Cooking time:
15–20 minutes
Freezing:
Recommended at
end of stage 3

1. Grease and line an 11 × 7 inch jelly roll pan and an
8 inch square shallow cake pan.
2. Place two-thirds of the sponge cake mixture in the jelly
roll pan and a third in the cake pan. Bake in a 350°F oven
for 15–20 minutes, until risen and springy to touch. Cool
the square cake on a rack.
3. Turn the jelly roll out onto lightly sugared paper. Trim
the edges, and spread with apricot glaze. Roll up firmly
and cool on a rack.
4. Color the icing red.

5. Cut a half slice, 1 inch thick, from one end of the jelly roll (Fig i).

6. Brush both jelly roll pieces with apricot glaze. Roll out half of the icing on a surface dusted with cornstarch, trim to size and fit around the jelly roll. Cover the cut-off piece and press in position on top of the engine for the cabin.

7. Cut the square cake into 6 equal-size pieces (Fig. ii) and sandwich together into 3 pairs for the freight wagons, using apricot glaze. Brush the surfaces with apricot glaze.

8. Roll out the remaining icing, trim and cover the sides of the wagons. Arrange the mini rolls side by side on one cake card and place the engine on top. Place the wagons on the other cake card.

Fig i

9. Coil a piece of liquorice to make a smoke funnel. Cut the 4 liquorice sticks in half, coil and press onto the wagons for wheels.

10. Coil 6 long liquorice pieces and place on the sides of the engine. Put a chocolate button in the middle of each. Use small candies to decorate the engine. Use the last 2 long pieces of liquorice to make railway tracks. Leave to dry.

11. Fill the wagons with banana chips, crystallized fruit and coated raisins.

Fig ii

SAIL BOAT

Make this as a birthday cake for anyone who enjoys sailing or as a *Bon Voyage* cake. Make a name plate and a flag from rice paper and a food color pen, if you wish.

3-egg quantity chocolate
 Quick Mix Cake
 *mixture**
2 teaspoons cocoa powder,
 blended with 2
 teaspoons boiling water
*1 quantity Butter Icing**
3 oz white ready-made
 marzipan
blue food color

1 bread stick
2 sheets rice paper
2 gumdrops
1 long piece of liquorice
3 candy cigarettes
4 mints
FINISHING TOUCHES:
8 × 6 inch cake card
jaw-breakers (optional)

Preparation time: 40 minutes plus making cake mixture and icing
Cooking time: 50–55 minutes
Freezing: Recommended at end of stage 2

1. Grease and line a 6½ × 3¾ × 3 inch loaf pan.
2. Turn the cake mixture into the pan and bake in a 325°F oven for 50–55 minutes, until well risen and springy to touch. Cool on a rack.
3. Trim the cake at one end to make a pointed bow and hollow out the top to make a slight depression (Fig i).
4. Beat the blended cocoa into two-thirds of the butter icing. Color remaining icing and marzipan pale blue.
5. Spread a thin layer of blue icing on the inside of the boat. Roll out the marzipan until large enough to fit inside the boat, place in position over the blue icing and trim.
6. Spread the top and sides of the boat with chocolate icing, using a palette knife dipped in hot water, and place on the cake card.
7. Spread the remaining blue icing over the cake card and peak it to look like the sea.
8. Trim the bread stick to an 8 inch length and press into the bow of the boat for the mast. Cut out 2 rice paper sails. Dampen the edges and stick to the mast.
9. Press 2 gumdrops onto the stern of the boat. Stick a strip of liquorice all around the outside of the boat. Cut the remaining liquorice lengthways into narrow strips and use some to trim the top of the boat.
10. Halve the cigarettes and press around the front of the boat. Attach a strip of liquorice with a little icing to these.
11. Thread 2 mints on remaining strips of liquorice for life savers and press onto each side. Place the jaw-breakers inside the boat to look like seats.

Fig i

Illustrated right bottom: Blue Racer (page 36)

RACING TRACK

Preparation time:
40 minutes plus
making cake
mixture and icing
Cooking time:
35–40 minutes
Freezing:
Recommended at
end of stage 2

Fig i

Fig ii

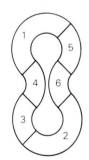

Fig iii

If you wish, make a flag using a cocktail stick and rice
paper, and mark with an edible food color pen.

*4-egg quantity chocolate
   Quick Mix Cake
   mixture**
*1 quantity chocolate
   Butter Icing**
*¼ cup flaked coconut
green, pink, blue, yellow
   and black food color
¼ lb jelly beans*

*11 white liquorice
   sandwich candies
3 oz ready-made white
   marzipan
8 liquorice centered
   candies
FINISHING TOUCH:
14 × 9 inch cake board*

1. Grease and line two 8 inch round cake pans.
2. Divide the cake mixture between the pans. Bake in a
325°F oven for 35–40 minutes, until risen and springy to
touch. Cool on a rack.
3. Using a plain cutter, cut a 3¼ inch circle from the
middle of each cake; cut one cake in half (Fig i) and the
other into quarters (Fig ii). Arrange on the cake board
according to Fig iii. Spread the top and sides with the icing.
4. Color the coconut green and use to coat the sides and
board. Arrange jelly beans around the edges.
5. Cut the white layer off 5 candies to show a liquorice
side, then arrange alternately with the white ones to mark
starting and finishing lines.
6. Cut the marzipan into 4 pieces. Color pink, yellow, blue
and black, and mold into racing cars. Halve the round
candies and position as wheels. Arrange on the race track.

BLUE RACER

Use a food color pen and rice paper for a license plate.

*3-egg quantity Quick Mix
   Cake mixture**
1 quantity Butter Icing*
*blue food color
2 mini chocolate rolls
1 piece of red liquorice
4 small cookies
8 thin strips of liquorice*

*1 filled liquorice roll
2 red gumdrops
large silver balls
¼ cup light brown
   granulated sugar
FINISHING TOUCH:
8 × 6 inch cake card*

1. Grease and line a 6½ × 3¾ × 3 inch loaf pan.

2. Place the cake mixture in the pan and bake in a 325°F oven for 50–55 minutes, until well risen and springy to touch. Cool on a rack.

3. Color the butter icing pale blue.

4. Cut 2 wedges from the cake (use for another recipe) to form a car shape (Fig i). Place the mini rolls on a cake board and position the cake on top. Spread the top and sides of the cake with icing, using a palette knife dipped in hot water.

5. Cut racing stripes and an aerial from the liquorice and place in position.

6. Spread the cookies with blue icing and place a liquorice strip around the edges. Press in position for the wheels. Cut the filled liquorice roll into 4 and press into the center of each wheel.

7. Cut 2 pieces from the liquorice strips for bumpers and press in position. Outline the doors and windows and make handles, wheel arches and wipers with liquorice strips, halved lengthways.

8. Position the gumdrops at the back for brake lights, and the silver balls for headlamps and a radiator grill.

9. Sprinkle brown sugar over the board for a track.

Preparation time: 45 minutes plus making cake mixture and icing
Cooking time: 50–55 minutes
Freezing: Recommended at end of stage 2

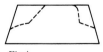

Fig i

Illustrated on page 35

CARAMEL CRISP CHICKS

¹/₄ lb caramels
2 tablespoons
 orange juice
2 oz puffed rice

1 teaspoon grated orange
 rind
2 oz ready-made yellow
 marzipan

Makes 15
Preparation time:
30 minutes
Freezing:
Not recommended

1. Place the caramels and orange juice in a pan and heat gently, stirring occasionally, until the caramel has melted. Remove from the heat and stir in the puffed rice and orange rind. Leave to cool for 2 minutes.
2. Using slightly wetted hands and working quickly, shape 15 tablespoonfuls of the mixture into chick-shape bodies with pointed tails, and 15 teaspoonfuls into round heads with pointed beaks. Press the heads onto the bodies as you work. Set aside.
3. Shape small pieces of marzipan into 15 pairs of wings and attach to the chicks. Mold 15 small beaks and 30 eyes from the remaining marzipan and press in position.

POPCORN MICE

If the marzipan is a little too dry to attach the features, use a little honey or Glacé Icing* instead.

1 tablespoon sunflower oil
2 oz popping corn
2 tablespoons flaked
 coconut
2 tablespoons sesame seeds

2 tablespoons honey
2 oz ready-made white
 marzipan
blue food color

Makes 15
Preparation time:
25 minutes
Freezing:
Not recommended

1. Heat the oil in a pan, add the corn, cover and cook gently until the corn has stopped popping; put in a bowl.
2. Mix together the coconut and sesame seeds.
3. Place the honey in the pan and bring to the boil. Remove from the heat, add the popcorn and half of the coconut mixture and mix well.
4. Take a tablespoon of the mixture and press firmly into a body shape with a pointed head, then toss in the remaining coconut mixture. Repeat to make 15 mice.
5. Color the marzipan pale blue: press out 30 ears and mold 30 eyes, 15 tails and 15 noses. Press in position.

HALLOWEEN HATS

1-egg quantity Beaten
   Sponge Cake mixture*
16 ice cream cones
½ lb ready-to-roll icing

black food color
2 tablespoons Apricot
   Glaze*
silver and gold food tint
   (optional)

Makes 16
Preparation time:
30 minutes plus
making sponge
cake mixture and
drying time
Cooking time:
10–15 minutes
Freezing:
Not recommended

1. Line 2 baking sheets with rice paper.
2. Place teaspoonfuls of the sponge mixture a little apart on the baking sheets and bake in a 350°F oven, for 10–15 minutes, until pale golden. Leave to cool on the baking sheets, then carefully separate by cutting around each cake.
3. Trim a 2 inch point off the end of each cone.
4. Reserve about 1 oz of the icing and color the remainder black.
5. Brush each cake and cone with apricot glaze.
6. Roll out the black icing very thinly on a surface dusted with cornstarch and cut out circles with a plain cutter to fit the cakes. Place on top and sides of the cakes.
7. Re-roll the icing trimmings and use to cover each cone. Position on the cakes with a little apricot glaze. Cut out star and moon shapes from the reserved white icing, brush with food tint if you wish, and position on the hats with a little apricot glaze. Leave for a few hours until dry.

PUMPKINS

*1-egg quantity orange
   Quick Mix Cake
   mixture**
*2 tablespoons Apricot
   Glaze**

*¹⁄₂ lb ready-to-roll icing
   green and orange food
   color*

1. Place 20 paper cake cases in muffin cups or on a baking sheet.

2. Divide the cake mixture between the cases and bake in a 325°F oven for 15–20 minutes, until well risen and springy to touch. Cool on a rack, then peel off the paper cases.

3. Sandwich pairs of cakes, tops together, with apricot glaze, then brush all over with apricot glaze.

4. Color a quarter of the icing green and the remainder orange.

5. Divide the orange icing into 10 pieces. Roll out thinly on a surface dusted with cornstarch and use to cover the cakes. Mold into a round shape with a dip in the top. Mark pumpkin lines with a knife, and features if you wish.

6. Press out 30 leaves from small balls of green icing and mark the veins with a knife; mold 10 stalks. Attach 3 leaves and a stalk to each pumpkin with apricot glaze. Leave for a few hours until dry.

Makes 10
Preparation time:
25 minutes plus making cake mixture and drying time
Cooking time:
15–20 minutes
Freezing:
Recommended at end of stage 2

COCOA CLOWNS

A crunchy cookie mixture made from banana chips, rice cereal and flaked coconut.

1/2 lb milk chocolate, melted
2 oz banana chips, crushed
2/3 cup flaked coconut
2 oz rice cereal
6 each red and green ice cream cones
4 sheets rice paper

18 each yogurt- and chocolate-coated raisins
little Glacé Icing* (optional)
2 oz ready-made white marzipan (approximately)
red and blue food color

Makes 12
Preparation time:
30 minutes
Freezing:
Not recommended

1. Line a baking sheet with waxed paper.
2. Mix half of the melted chocolate with the banana chips, coconut and rice cereal until well blended.
3. Half fill a small rounded egg cup with the mixture and press down well with the back of a teaspoon. Invert onto the baking sheet and tap firmly to remove. Repeat to make 12 'heads'.
4. Place a 2½ inch plain cutter on the baking sheet. Place 1 tablespoon of the mixture inside the cutter and press down firmly. Remove the cutter and repeat to make 12 circles. Leave to set.
5. Brush the heads and the top and side of the circles with chocolate, warming to melt again if necessary.
6. Trim a 2½ inch pointed end from each cone to represent the hats, discarding the wide sections.
7. Cut 12 fluted circles of rice paper to fit over the biscuit circles, and 12 smaller circles to fit under the 'hats', using 3 inch and 1 inch fluted cutters as guides.
8. Assemble the clowns as follows, securing the pieces with melted chocolate: stick 1 large rice paper frill on top of each chocolate circle, then attach the head, a smaller frill and finally the hat. Stick 3 coated raisins onto each hat, alternating the colors.
9. Pipe 24 arches for eyebrows using glacé icing or mold from a little white marzipan. Color half the marzipan blue and half red. Make 12 red noses and 12 mouths. Shape 24 blue circles for eyes. Place in position, securing with chocolate.

CHOCOLATE WHEAT RABBITS

Coat these rabbits with milk, semi-sweet or white chocolate or, if you prefer, use carob.

¹/₄ cup dried apricots
¹/₃ cup raisins
4 fresh dates, pitted
¹/₂ cup wheat flakes
1 tablespoon lemon juice

3 oz baker's semi-sweet
*   chocolate, melted*
2 oz ready-made white
*   marzipan*
20 slivered almonds

1. Very finely chop the apricots, raisins and dates. Place in
a bowl and add the wheat flakes and lemon juice. Form the
mixture into 10 firm balls, then press into oval rabbit
shapes. Place on a rack over a plate.
2. Mold 20 eyes, and 10 noses and tails from the white
marzipan.
3. Spoon the melted chocolate over each rabbit. Position
the marzipan features on each rabbit and press the
almonds in position for ears.
4. Leave to set.

Makes 10
Preparation time:
20 minutes
Freezing:
Not recommended

SNOWMEN

2²/₃ cups flaked coconut
¹/₃ cup condensed milk
4 round candies with
   liquorice centers

9 solid liquorice rolls
2 pieces of liquorice
colored balls

Makes 12
Preparation time:
20 minutes
Cooking time:
10 minutes
Freezing:
Not recommended

1. Place the coconut and 4 tablespoons of the condensed milk in a bowl and mix together until evenly blended.
2. Fill a small rounded egg cup with the coconut mixture, pressing down well. Tap firmly to remove and place on a lightly floured baking sheet. Repeat to make 12 bodies.
3. Form the remaining mixture into 12 small balls and place on the bodies, securing with condensed milk.
4. Bake in a 300°F oven for 10 minutes, until set but not browned. Cool on a rack.
5. Cut each round candy into 3 slices and place half a liquorice roll on each candy to make hats. Place in position and secure with condensed milk.
6. Make liquorice buttons from the 3 remaining rolls and cut lengths of liquorice strip for scarves; use the colored balls to represent eyes and noses: position, using more condensed milk if necessary.

CHRISTMAS TREES

3 tablespoons creamed
   honey
2 tablespoons butter
1¹/₂ cups whole wheat
   flour
2 teaspoons baking
   powder
1 teaspoon mixed spice

1 tablespoon milk
1 egg yolk
¹/₂ lb ready-made white
   marzipan
green food color
2 tablespoons Apricot
   Glaze*
colored balls

1. Place the honey and butter in a saucepan and heat gently, stirring occasionally, until melted. Remove from the heat and stir in the flour, baking powder, mixed spice, milk and egg yolk. Mix to a soft dough, then knead on a lightly floured surface until smooth.
2. Roll out the dough thinly and cut out 9 Christmas trees using a shaped cutter. Cut 3 tree shapes in half lengthways.
3. Arrange all the shapes on 2 lightly floured baking sheets and bake in a 350°F oven for 10 minutes, or until lightly browned. Transfer carefully to a rack to cool.

4. Color the marzipan a rich green. Roll out very thinly on a sugared surface and cut out 12 Christmas tree shapes; cut 6 in half lengthways.

5. Brush the front of each whole cookie and both sides of each half cookie with a little apricot glaze, then position the marzipan shapes on top.

6. Brush the straight edge of the half-tree shapes with a little apricot glaze. Press each half at right angles onto the center of the whole tree cookies so that they stand up.

7. Secure the balls at the points of each tree with a little apricot glaze.

Makes 6
Preparation time:
25 minutes
Cooking time:
10 minutes
Freezing:
Not recommended

UMBRELLAS AND CANES

Bright colorful cookies flavored with orange rind.

⅓ cup margarine
¼ cup superfine sugar
1 teaspoon grated orange
  rind
1 egg white

1¼ cups self-rising flour
1 oz pudding mix
pink, yellow and green
  food color

Makes 24
Preparation time:
30 minutes
Cooking time:
5–8 minutes
Freezing:
Recommended

1. Line 2 baking sheets with waxed paper.
2. Beat the margarine and sugar together until light and fluffy. Beat in the orange rind and egg white until smooth, then sift in the flour and pudding mix and mix to a soft dough.
3. Divide the dough into 3 pieces and color pink, yellow and green. Cut each piece in half. Take one portion of each colored dough, break into pieces and roll into 5 inch pencil-thin lengths using a flat hand.
4. Take 2 lengths of different colored dough and twist gently together, then curl the end to form a handle. Repeat to make about 12 canes. Place on a baking sheet.
5. Roll out each piece of the remaining dough and cut out two 2¾ inch circles from each using a plain cutter to give 6 circles. Cut each circle in half. Using the end of a ½ inch plain piping tip, cut out 4 semi-circles from the straight edge of each semi-circle of dough to make umbrella shapes.
6. Knead each color trimmings together. Roll into 2 inch lengths using a flat hand, and make 12 handles as before. Place on a baking sheet and position the umbrella shapes, pressing gently to join. Roll any remaining dough into beads and decorate the umbrellas.
7. Bake in a 350°F oven for 5–8 minutes, until just tinged at the edges. Transfer carefully to a rack to cool.

BUTTERFLIES

Use any food color to paint these cookies.

1¼ cups sifted all-purpose
  flour
¼ cup fine oatmeal
⅓ cup butter

3 tablespoons superfine
  sugar
1 egg, separated
blue and pink food color
*2 oz Butter Icing**

1. Place the flour and oatmeal in a bowl. Rub in the butter until the mixture resembles breadcrumbs. Stir in the sugar and egg white and mix to a firm dough.

2. Turn out onto a lightly floured surface and knead until smooth. Roll out thinly and cut out about 44 butterflies using a shaped cutter.

3. Arrange half of the shapes on a lightly greased baking sheet and bake in a 350°F oven for 8–10 minutes or until lightly browned. Carefully transfer to a rack to cool.

4. Meanwhile, cut the remaining butterfly shapes in half to make wings. Divide the egg yolk in half and color blue and pink. Using a fine paintbrush, outline each cut wing with blue egg glaze. Clean the brush well, then glaze the center of each wing with pink glaze.

5. Bake in the oven for about 8 minutes, until the cookies are cooked and the glaze is bright. Cool on a rack.

6. Carefully spread a thin line of butter icing down the center of each butterfly and press the wings gently in position.

Makes 22
Preparation time:
20 minutes plus
making icing
Cooking time:
About 18 minutes
Freezing:
Recommended

CRACKER COTTAGE

Just like a dessert cake, but savory instead of sweet.

*3 hard-boiled eggs,
   chopped finely
7 oz can tuna in oil,
   drained
1 tablespoon mayonnaise
2 × 6 oz packs rectangular
   crackers
1½ cups cream cheese
4 large slices whole wheat
   bread
2 tablespoons plain yogurt*

*4 oz package cheese
   buttons
2 oz package Japanese
   assorted rice crackers
2 celery sticks, cut into strips
½ green pepper, cored,
   seeded and cut into
   squares
1 carrot, cut into 2
   rectangles
2 tablespoons chopped
   parsley*

Serves 16
Preparation time:
30 minutes
Freezing:
Not recommended

1. Mix together the eggs, tuna and mayonnaise.
2. Arrange 6 crackers on a board and spread with the tuna mixture. Top with another 6 crackers. Repeat until there are 8 layers of crackers. Top with a thin layer of cream cheese.
3. Make 2 sandwiches with the bread and some of the cream cheese. Cut off the crusts and cut each sandwich into 8 triangles. Arrange in 2 rows on top of the crackers to make a double pitched roof.
4. Blend together the rest of the cream cheese and yogurt and spread carefully over the roof and sides of the cottage.
5. Tile the roof with cheese buttons, starting at the long edge and working up to the top on each side.
6. Press the Japanese crackers around the base of the cottage and under the eaves, and use one for a chimney.
7. Use the celery for shutters, the green pepper for windows, and the carrot for doors.
8. Sprinkle the board with parsley and make a cheese button path and a cracker border. Serve immediately.

SNAKES AND LADDERS

2 strips bacon
1/2 cup whole wheat flour
1/2 cup sifted all-purpose
white flour
1/4 cup margarine
1 egg, separated

1 tablespoon tomato paste
2 tablespoons pumpkin
seeds
4 raisins
pepper to taste

Makes 12
Preparation time:
20 minutes
Cooking time:
15 minutes
Freezing:
Recommended

1. Broil the bacon until crisp, then chop finely.
2. Place the flours in a bowl and rub in the margarine until the mixture resembles breadcrumbs. Stir in the bacon, pepper and egg white and mix to a firm dough.
3. Knead lightly on a floured surface until smooth, then cut into 3 pieces.
4. Using a flat hand, roll one piece into a thin roll about 16 inches long. Cut into 4 equal lengths and form each into a snake shape. Repeat with another piece of dough to make 4 more snakes. Place on a lightly floured baking sheet.
5. Roll the remaining piece of dough into a longer, thinner roll and cut into eight 3 inch lengths. Place in pairs a little apart on the baking sheet.
6. Knead the trimmings together and roll into an even thinner roll for the rungs. Place in position to make the ladders.
7. Mix the egg yolk and tomato paste together and brush over the snakes and ladders.
8. Press pumpkin seeds along the top of each snake and in one end for a tongue. Cut the raisins into small pieces and use for eyes.
9. Bake in a 350°F oven for 15 minutes, until golden. Cool on a rack.

CLOCK QUICHE

1 cup whole wheat flour
1 cup sifted all-purpose
white flour
1/2 cup margarine
3 tablespoons cold water
FOR THE FILLING:
1 potato
1 zucchini
1 carrot

2 teaspoons sunflower oil
2 scallions, chopped
1/2 cup grated Cheddar
cheese
3 eggs
2/3 cup milk
salt and pepper to taste
parsley sprig to garnish

1. Place the flours in a bowl and rub in the margarine until the mixture resembles breadcrumbs. Stir in the water and mix to a firm dough.

2. Knead on a lightly floured surface until smooth, then roll out thinly and use to line a 10 inch fluted dish. Prick the base and chill while making the numbers.

3. Knead the pastry trimmings together and roll out thinly. Cut out numbers 1 to 12 using numeral cutters, or roll out pencil-thin strips of pastry and shape into numbers. Also cut out large and small hands for the clock. Place on a baking sheet.

4. Line the pastry case with waxed paper and fill with baking beans. Bake the case, numbers and hands in a 400°F oven for 10–15 minutes. Remove the paper and beans. Lower the temperature to 325°F.

5. Meanwhile, grate the vegetables finely. Heat the oil in a pan, add the grated vegetables and scallions and cook for 3 minutes, until almost tender. Place in the pastry case and sprinkle with the cheese.

6. Beat together the eggs, milk, and salt and pepper and pour into the pastry case. Arrange the numbers evenly around the quiche, with the hands in the center.

7. Return to the oven for 25 minutes or until the filling has set. Serve warm or cold, garnished with parsley.

Serves 12
Preparation time:
25 minutes
Cooking time:
35–40 minutes
Freezing:
Recommended

WOODLAND TOADSTOOLS

6 medium hard-boiled
  eggs
2 oz fine liver paté
12 round crackers
6 small tomatoes, halved
  and seeded

1 carton mustard and
  cress or alfalfa sprouts
1 triangle cheese spread (at
  room temperature)

Makes 12
Preparation time:
25 minutes
Freezing:
Not recommended

1. Cut each egg in half widthways, carefully scoop out the yolks and place in a bowl with the paté. Beat together, then spoon three-quarters of this mixture into the egg whites.
2. Spread the crackers with the remaining paté mixture and top each with an egg half, rounded side up. Place a tomato half on top and sprinkle mustard and cress or alfalfa sprouts around the base.
3. Place the cheese spread in a waxed paper piping bag, snip off the end, and pipe dots onto the tomatoes.

HAPPY HATS

1 cup whole wheat flour
1½ teaspoons baking
  powder
¼ teaspoon dry mustard
¼ cup margarine
½ cup finely grated
  Cheddar cheese
1 egg, beaten
1–2 tablespoons water

salt and pepper to taste
FOR THE TOPPING:
12 slices processed cheese
12 cherry tomatoes
butter to spread
24 blades of chive or strips
  of scallion
parsley sprigs

Makes 24
Preparation time:
25 minutes
Cooking time:
15 minutes
Freezing:
Recommended at
end of stage 3

1. Place the flour, baking powder, mustard, and salt and pepper in a bowl. Rub in the margarine until the mixture resembles breadcrumbs, then stir in the grated cheese, egg and enough water to mix to a firm dough.
2. Knead on a lightly floured surface until smooth, then roll out thinly and cut out 24 circles using a 1¾ inch fluted cutter.
3. Place on 2 lightly floured baking sheets and bake in a 350°F oven for 15 minutes, until lightly browned. Cool.
4. Using the same cutter, cut out 2 circles from each cheese slice. Cut each tomato in half.
5. Spread the crackers with a little butter and place a cheese circle and half tomato on top. Tie a blade of chive or scallion around the base of each tomato and arrange a tiny parsley sprig at the side.

SESAME NUMERALS

So easy to make—the children could help.

1½ *cups whole wheat*
  flour
2 *teaspoons baking*
  powder

½ *cup margarine*
1 *teaspoon curry paste*
1 *egg, separated*
3 *tablespoons sesame seeds*

Makes about 22
Preparation time:
15 minutes
Cooking time:
15–20 minutes
Freezing:
Recommended

1. Place the flour and baking powder in a bowl and rub in the margarine until the mixture resembles breadcrumbs.
2. Blend the curry paste and egg yolk together, then work into the mixture to form a firm dough.
3. Knead lightly on a floured surface until smooth, then cut into 4 pieces. Using a flat hand, roll one piece at a time into a long thin roll, about 20 inches long. Cut each roll into about 5 inch lengths and shape into numbers 0–9. Use any trimmings to make + and = shapes, if you wish.
4. Lightly beat the egg white and brush the top of each number. Sprinkle with the sesame seeds and arrange on 2 lightly floured baking sheets.
5. Bake in a 350°F oven for 15–20 minutes, until lightly browned. Cool on a rack.

TIC-TAC-TOE PIZZAS

Quickly made using a package mix, but try your own favorite bread recipe if you have more time.

2 *tablespoons vegetable oil*
1 *onion, chopped finely*
1 *lb tomatoes, skinned and*
  chopped
1½ *tablespoons tomato*
  paste

2 *teaspoons chopped basil*
2 × 5 *oz packages pizza*
  base mix
8 *oz package processed*
  cheese slices
salt and pepper to taste

1. Heat 2 teaspoons of the oil in a pan, add the onion and cook for 2 minutes, stirring occasionally, until tender.
2. Stir in the tomatoes, tomato paste, basil, and salt and pepper. Bring to the boil slowly, then cook briskly until thick and pulpy. Leave to cool.
3. Make up the pizza bases according to package directions, then cut in half.
4. Roll out and trim one piece to an 8 inch square. Cut the square into 4 and place on a lightly floured baking sheet. Brush the squares with a little of the remaining oil and

cover with tomato mixture. Repeat with the second piece of dough.

5. Bake in a 425°F oven for 15 minutes.

6. Cut the cheese slices into 8 strips. Arrange 4 on each square to mark the tic-tac-toe grid. Return to the oven for about 5 minutes, until the cheese just melts.

7. Meanwhile, using a flat hand, roll the dough trimmings into pencil-thin lengths. Cut into short strips for the 'X's' and shape into circles for the 'O's'. Place on a floured baking sheet and bake in the oven for 10 minutes, or until crisp. Cool on a rack.

8. Serve the pizzas warm or cold, with 'X's' and 'O's' handed separately so the children can play their own game.

Makes 8
Preparation time:
30 minutes
Cooking time:
About 20 minutes
Freezing:
Recommended

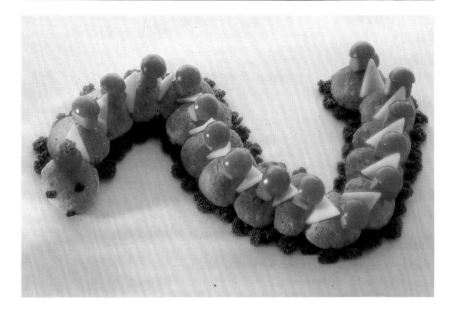

HISSING SID

10 oz package whole wheat bread mix	Edam cheese cut into triangular slices
3 raisins	5 frankfurters
1/4 cup butter	8 cherry tomatoes, halved
2 cloves garlic, crushed	parsley sprigs to garnish

Serves 16
Preparation time: 25 minutes, plus rising dough
Cooking time: About 20 minutes
Freezing: Recommended at end of stage 5

1. Make up the bread mix according to package directions.
2. Divide the dough into 16 pieces and shape 14 into round balls. Arrange them on a floured baking sheet in an 'S' shape.
3. Shape the remaining 2 pieces into a head and tail and attach at each end of the snake. Mark the eyes and mouth with raisins, cover with plastic wrap and leave to rise in a warm place for 15–20 minutes, until doubled in size.
4. Bake in a 450°F oven for 15–20 minutes, until well risen and lightly browned.
5. Beat the butter and garlic together. Cut in between each join in the snake, but do not slice right through. Spread the cut surfaces with garlic butter. Wrap in foil and return to the oven for 5 minutes.
6. Just before serving, place a cheese slice in between the joins. Cut the frankfurters into pieces and spear onto cocktail sticks with the tomato halves: push into the bread. Garnish with parsley to serve.

CRISPY BOYS AND GIRLS

1 cup self-rising flour
¼ teaspoon dry mustard
¼ cup margarine
1 teaspoon grated onion
1 cup grated sharp
   Cheddar cheese
1 egg white

salt and pepper to taste
TO FINISH:
1 egg yolk
1 teaspoon tomato paste
1 tablespoon currants
2 tablespoons pine nuts

1. Sift the flour, mustard, and salt and pepper into a bowl. Rub in the margarine until the mixture resembles bread-crumbs. Stir in the onion, half of the cheese, and the egg white to form a firm dough.

2. Knead on a lightly floured surface until smooth, then roll out thinly and cut out 6 girls and 6 boys using gingerbread cutters. Arrange on lightly floured baking sheets.

3. Brush the faces with egg yolk. Blend the remaining yolk with the tomato paste and brush over the bodies.

4. Sprinkle the remaining cheese over the pants and skirts. Mark the eyes, noses, hair and belts with currants and pine nuts.

5. Bake in a 350°F oven for 10 minutes or until golden brown. Transfer carefully to a rack. Serve warm or cold.

Makes 12
Preparation time:
20 minutes
Cooking time:
10 minutes
Freezing:
Recommended

NOVELTY ROLLS

1 quantity Bread Dough*   *1 tablespoon currants*
1 egg, beaten

Makes 16
Preparation time:
25–30 minutes
plus making
dough
Cooking time:
15–20 minutes
Freezing:
Recommended

1. Re-knead the dough and divide into 16 pieces. Form them into any of the following shapes:-
Fish: Shape a piece of dough into a flat oval shape. Cut a 'V' from one end for the tail and snip from the tail to the head with scissors to make the 'scales'.
Rabbit: Cut a piece of dough in half. Shape one half into a round body. Shape a head from half of the remaining piece and place in position. Shape 2 ears and a tail from the rest and place in position.
Snake: Using a flat hand, roll a piece of dough into a thin roll, about 6 inches long. Bend into a snake shape and make a row of small snips along its back with scissors.
Hedgehog: Roll a piece of dough into a circle with a pointed end. Using scissors, snip the dough all over to make 'spines'.
Ladybug: Take a piece of dough, remove a piece the size of a filbert and roll into a ball. Shape the larger piece into a dome and position the ball at the front. Make a shallow cut along the center to represent wings.
Mouse: Cut a quarter off a piece of dough. Shape the rest into a round body with a slightly pointed nose. Press out 2 ears and roll a thin tail from the remaining piece and attach to the body.
Snail: Cut a quarter off a piece of dough and shape into a head. Using a flat hand, roll the remaining piece into a long thin length and make a coil, leaving the end piece for the tail. Press the head in position.
2. Place the 'animals' on a floured baking sheet, cover with plastic wrap and leave to rise in a warm place for 10–15 minutes. Brush with beaten egg and press on currants to represent features.
3. Bake in a 425°F oven for 15–20 minutes, until golden. Cool on a rack.

PORCUPINES

½ cup cream cheese   *4 tablespoons pumpkin*
½ cup finely grated   *seeds*
Cheddar cheese   *1 tablespoon currants*
4 cheese thin crackers,
crushed finely

1. Mix the cheeses together, stir in the cracker crumbs and mix well.
2. Take a teaspoonful of mixture at a time and roll into a ball, using wetted hands if the mixture sticks. Place on a board and shape the nose to make a porcupine.
3. Press the pumpkin seeds into each porcupine for the spines. Cut the currants into tiny pieces and use to mark the eyes and nose. Chill until required.

Makes 20
Preparation time:
20 minutes
Freezing:
Not recommended

VARIATIONS
1. Flavor the cream cheese with chopped dried fruit.
2. Add a little crushed garlic, curry powder or tomato paste to the mixture for slightly older children who like a bit of extra flavor.

FESTIVE NOVELTY IDEAS

FESTIVE FANCIES

*1-egg quantity
    Gingerbread Dough**
*2 tablespoons Apricot
    Glaze**
*1 lb ready-to-roll icing
    colored balls*

*red, green and yellow food
    color*
1 quantity Royal Icing*
FINISHING TOUCH:
*1 yard each of ⅛ inch
    wide green and red
    ribbon*

Makes 18
Preparation time:
1 hour plus
making dough and
icing, and drying
time
Cooking time:
10–15 minutes
Freezing:
Not recommended

1. Roll out the dough thinly on a lightly floured surface and cut out 6 squares, 6 ovals and 6 hearts with 2 inch plain or fluted cutters. Arrange on 2 lightly floured baking sheets and make a hole in the top of each, using a straw.
2. Bake in a 350°F oven for 10–15 minutes or until browned at the edges. Cool on a rack. When cold, brush with apricot glaze.
3. Roll out the ready-to-roll icing thinly on a surface sprinkled with cornstarch and cut out shapes to match the cookies. Place on the cookies and cut out the holes.
4. Outline the hearts with colored balls.
5. Color a quarter of the icing trimmings red and roll out thinly. Cut out 6 small hearts and place in the center of each heart cookie. Use the trimmings to make about 100 tiny holly berries and set aside.
6. Color three-quarters of the remaining icing trimmings green and cut out 36 small and 30 large holly leaves (see page 78).
7. Mold 6 Christmas roses from the remaining icing trimmings (see pages 78–79) and leave to dry.
8. Arrange 6 small holly leaves and several berries around the edge of each oval shape with a Christmas rose in the center, securing with a little royal icing.
9. Place the large holly leaves and remaining berries in clusters of 5 at the corner of each square biscuit. Place half of the royal icing in a piping bag fitted with a writing tip and pipe a name or greeting. Over-pipe with the remaining royal icing, colored red or green.

Illustrated bottom
right: Picture
Cookies (page 62)

10. Leave the cookies to dry, then thread lengths of ribbon through the holes. Wrap in plastic wrap to keep fresh, then hang up or give as presents.

PICTURE COOKIES

1 quantity Cookie Dough*
1 quantity Royal Icing*
FINISHING TOUCHES:
food color pens of various
    colors

1 yard each of ⅛ inch
    wide pink, green and
    red ribbon

Makes 24
Preparation time:
45 minutes plus
making dough and
icing, and drying
time
Cooking time:
8–10 minutes
Freezing:
Not recommended

Illustrated on
page 61

1. Roll out the dough thinly on a lightly floured surface and cut out 24 shapes using assorted 2¼ inch plain and fluted cookie cutters. Arrange on 2 lightly floured baking sheets and make a hole in the top of each, using a straw.
2. Bake in a 350°F oven for 8–10 minutes, until just beginning to color at the edges. Cool on a rack.
3. Spread the royal icing evenly over each cookie. Leave to dry, then draw on Christmas trees, lanterns, snowmen, holly leaves and berries, etc, or write messages, with food color pens.
4. Thread lengths of ribbon through the holes. Wrap the cookies in plastic wrap to keep fresh, then hang up or give as Christmas presents.

ANGELIC APPLES

A toffee apple choir and angels which children will love.

6 small eating apples
6 wooden sticks
½ cup water
¾ cup light brown sugar,
    packed
2 tablespoons golden syrup
    or 1 tablespoon each
    light corn syrup and
    molasses

2 tablespoons butter
½ teaspoon lemon juice
6 colored chocolate
    candies, halved
1 oz ready-made white
    marzipan, colored red
8 sheets rice paper
6 small paper cups

1. Wash and dry the apples thoroughly; press a stick a third of the way into each.
2. Place the water, sugar and syrup in a saucepan and heat gently, stirring occasionally, until the sugar has completely dissolved.
3. Add the butter and lemon juice and boil rapidly until the syrup reaches 260°F on a candy thermometer and is beginning to turn a darker brown. If you do not have a candy thermometer, test by adding a drop of syrup to some cold water: a hard ball should form. Remove from

the heat and allow the bubbles to subside.

4. Tilt the pan and dip an apple quickly into the toffee, then place on a baking sheet lined with waxed paper, allowing a pool of toffee to form at the base. Press chocolate candies in position for eyes. Mold mouths from red marzipan and position. Repeat with the other 5 apples. If the toffee begins to set in the pan, heat gently.

5. *To make choir boys:* cut a circle of rice paper ½ inch larger than the base of the cups. Place on the base and press the toffee apple in position, with the stick going through the cup. Cover the cups with rice paper, trim the edges and dampen to stick in position. Make a small rice paper song sheet and stick in position.

6. *To make angels:* cover the cups with rice paper as above and insert the toffee apples. Cut out rice paper wings, circles for heads and a candle and stick in position.

7. Wrap the toffee apples separately in plastic wrap to store.

Makes 6
Preparation time:
35 minutes
Cooking time:
5 minutes
Freezing:
Not recommended

BREAD ORNAMENTS

If you prefer to eat these Christmas decorations then you may do so within 24 hours of making—they make lovely croutons for soup. Alternatively they may be hung up in a dry, warm atmosphere throughout the festive season.

1 quantity Bread Dough*
1 egg, beaten
about 2 tablespoons each
*   sesame and poppy seeds*

FINISHING TOUCH:
2 yards each of ⅛ wide
*   green and red ribbon*

Makes about 30
Preparation time:
20 minutes plus
making dough
Cooking time:
8–10 minutes
Freezing:
Recommended

1. Re-knead the dough for 1 minute, then roll out very thinly on a floured surface. Using small cookie cutters, cut out a variety of shapes and place on a floured baking sheet. Make a hole at the top of each one, using a straw.

2. Brush the shapes with egg, sprinkle some with seeds, and bake in a 425°F oven for 8–10 minutes, until puffy and golden brown.

3. Cool on a rack, then thread with lengths of ribbon and hang on the tree.

HOLLY WREATH

1 quantity Bread Dough*   *1 egg, beaten*

1. Re-knead the dough for 1 minute, until smooth. Cut off about a quarter and set aside for decoration.
2. Using a flat hand, roll the remaining dough into a roll about 24 inches long. Bring the ends together. Place on a lightly floured baking sheet, cover with plastic wrap and leave to rise in a warm place for 20 minutes.
3. Meanwhile, roll out the remaining dough very thinly on a floured surface and cut out about 40 holly leaves, using a cutter or a sharp knife. Mark on veins and place on a floured plate. Roll about 40 small beads of dough for the berries and place on the plate. Cover with plastic wrap.
4. Bake the ring in a 425°F oven for 10–15 minutes, until pale golden.
5. Arrange the holly leaves, overlapping, and the berries, in clusters, all around the ring and brush with egg glaze.
6. Return to the oven and cook for 5–6 minutes, until the decorations are crisp but not brown. Cool on a rack. Hang with a wide ribbon or use as a table centerpiece.

Makes one
Preparation time:
30 minutes plus making dough
Cooking time:
15–21 minutes
Freezing:
Recommended

STAINED GLASS WINDOW

*1 quantity Cookie Dough***	*FINISHING TOUCH:*
1 egg yolk	*1 yard each of $\frac{1}{8}$ inch*
red and green food color	*wide red and green*
$\frac{1}{2}$ lb fruit drops	*ribbon*

Makes about 12
Preparation time:
35 minutes plus
making dough
Cooking time:
8–10 minutes
Freezing:
Not recommended

1. Roll out the dough thinly on a lightly floured surface. Cut into 8 rectangles 4 × 2½ inches and place apart on 2 baking sheets lined with waxed paper.
2. Cut off the 2 top corners of each rectangle and shape into a dome to represent a church window.
3. Using small cutters, cut out 3 shapes from each window. Knead all the trimmings together, roll out and use to make more windows; place on a baking sheet.
4. Divide the egg yolk into 2 and color red and green. Using a soft glazing brush, brush the window frames evenly with the egg glaze.
5. Cut the fruit drops in half and place a different colored one in each cut-out shape. Make a small hole in the top of each window, using a drinking straw.
6. Bake in a 350°F oven for 8–10 minutes, until the candies have melted and filled the shapes, and the cookies are just coloring at the edges. Leave on the paper until cold, then remove carefully.
7. Thread a length of ribbon through the top of each window. Wrap in plastic wrap to keep fresh, then hang up or give as presents.

LANTERNS

It really is worth the time and effort to make these pretty Christmas lanterns.

1-egg quantity	*FINISHING TOUCH:*
*Gingerbread Dough***	*1 yard each of $\frac{1}{8}$ inch*
8 each red and green fruit	*wide green and red*
drops	*ribbon*
2 teaspoons water	

1. Roll out the dough thinly on a floured surface and cut out 24 squares using a 1¾ inch fluted square cookie cutter. Arrange on 2 baking sheets lined with waxed paper.
2. Carefully cut out the center of each square with a small cutter or sharp knife and remove, leaving a ¼ inch frame. Knead all the trimmings together.

3. Cut 6 red and 6 green fruit drops in half and place a piece in the center of each frame. Bake in a 350°F oven for 8–10 minutes, until the candies have melted and filled the frames. Leave until cold, then carefully peel off the paper.

4. Roll out the trimmings and cut out 12 squares using a 2¼ inch square fluted cookie cutter. Using the wide end of a ½ inch plain piping tip cut out 12 circles from the remaining trimmings, then cut out the centers with the narrow end. Place the squares and rings on a lightly floured baking sheet and bake as before.

5. Place the remaining red candies and a teaspoon of water in a bowl over a pan of boiling water until melted.

6. Using a cocktail stick, spread the edges of 4 red cookies with the melted candies and press together to make a square. Attach a square cookie to the top and bottom. Stick 2 ring cookies together and attach to the top of the lantern with melted candy. Repeat to make 2 more red lanterns.

7. Make 3 green lanterns in the same way.

8. Attach the ribbons and wrap in plastic wrap to store.

Makes 6
Preparation time: 50 minutes plus making dough
Cooking time: 16–20 minutes
Freezing: Not recommended

SUGAR BASKETS

*1 quantity Quick Molding
Icing**
pink food color

*FINISHING TOUCHES:
pink tissue paper
2 yards of ¼ inch wide
white ribbon*

Makes 8
Preparation time:
50 minutes plus
making icing and
drying time
Freezing:
Not recommended

1. Reserve a piece of icing the size of a walnut for attaching the handles. Color half of the icing pale pink.
2. Roll out an eighth of the pink icing on a surface sprinkled with cornstarch and cut into seven 5 × ½ inch strips. Repeat with an eighth of the white icing.
3. Thread 6 pink and 6 white strips closely together to make a basket weave. Trim to a square. Place over a tumbler sprinkled thickly with cornstarch to shape, and trim to form a round basket. Leave in a warm place to dry.
4. Twist together the 2 remaining strips of icing, then curve to make a handle. Repeat with the remaining icing to make another 7 baskets and handles. Leave to dry.
5. Secure the handles to the baskets with little pieces of reserved icing. Arrange some tissue paper inside the baskets and fill with a gift, Miniature Eggs (opposite) or other candy. Tie pretty bows on the handles.

MINIATURE EGGS

*¼ lb ready-made white
    marzipan*
*24 large whole almonds,
    blanched and dried*

*6 oz ready-to-roll icing
pink, blue and yellow food
    color*
*1 quantity Royal Icing**

1. Divide the marzipan into 24 pieces and mold each piece around an almond. Leave in a warm place.
2. Cut the ready-to-roll icing into 3 equal-size pieces. Tint one piece pale pink, another piece pale blue and remaining piece pale yellow.
3. Cut each piece of colored icing into 8 even-size pieces. Using fingers dusted with cornstarch, press out one piece at a time and wrap around each marzipan almond, pressing joins together. Place on a plate and leave to dry in a warm place.
4. Half-fill a waxed paper piping bag, fitted with a No 1 plain writing tip, with royal icing. Fold down top securely.
5. Pipe decorations on each miniature egg e.g. tiny beads, lines, names or messages. Leave in a warm place to dry, then pack into pretty boxes or use to fill Sugar Baskets (opposite) for Easter presents.

Makes 24
Preparation time:
45 minutes plus
making icing and
drying time
Freezing:
Not recommended

CHOCOLATE EASTER EGG

6 oz semi-sweet, milk or white chocolate, melted	5 small fresh flowers
2–3 tiny rose leaves	1 egg white, beaten
	superfine sugar

Makes 1 medium-size chocolate egg
Preparation time: 30 minutes plus setting time
Freezing: Not recommended

1. Brush the inside of 2 Easter egg molds with a layer of melted chocolate; leave to set. Repeat to give 3 layers of chocolate; leave to set hard.
2. Brush the underside of each rose leaf with a layer of chocolate. Leave to set, then peel off each rose leaf carefully.
3. Brush each flower evenly with egg white, then cover with sugar. Leave to dry completely on a rack covered with paper towels in a warm place.
4. Carefully remove the egg from the mold by pressing the top. Fill if you wish, then brush the edges with melted chocolate and stick the shells together.
5. Place the remaining chocolate in a waxed paper piping bag fitted with a star tip and pipe a row of shells around the join.
6. Attach the flowers and chocolate leaves to the egg with melted chocolate and leave for 30 minutes to set. Wrap in plastic wrap, or place in a box.

MARZIPAN EGGS

8 oz package ready-made white marzipan	2 oz baker's semi-sweet chocolate, melted
pink, yellow and blue food color	8 pistachio nuts, finely chopped

Makes 20
Preparation time: 30 minutes plus setting time
Freezing: Not recommended

1. Divide the marzipan into 20 even-size pieces and tint 12 of them: 4 pale pink, 4 pale yellow and 4 pale blue. Cut off a piece the size of a pea from each portion and roll into long thin strips.
2. Shape each colored piece of marzipan into an egg shape. Use the marzipan strips to tie a bow of a contrasting color around each egg.
3. Mold the remaining 8 pieces of marzipan into egg shapes. Dip in the melted chocolate to coat and sprinkle with pistachio nuts.
4. Leave in a dry place for 1 hour to set, then pack into pretty boxes or Easter Nests (opposite).

EASTER NESTS

1 quantity Bread Dough*   *1 egg, beaten, to glaze*

1. Re-knead the dough for 1 minute, then divide into 24 pieces. Using a flat hand, roll 3 pieces into 8 inch long rolls, then braid together evenly. Cut off the ends to neaten, then join to make a ring. Press the trimmings into a thin round base about 1 inch across.

2. Press the braided ring onto the base to make a nest and place on a lightly floured baking sheet. Repeat to make 7 more nests. Cover with plastic wrap and leave to rise in a warm place for 10 minutes or until plump.

3. Brush with beaten egg, prick the bases and bake in a 425°F oven for 15–20 minutes, until golden brown. Remove from the baking sheet and cool on a rack.

4. Serve for breakfast or fill with bought candy or Marzipan Eggs (opposite).

Makes 8
Preparation time: 20 minutes plus making dough
Cooking time: 15–20 minutes
Freezing: Recommended at end of stage 3

SUGAR EASTER EGGS

1 quantity Quick Molding Icing*	FINISHING TOUCH (optional)
yellow and blue food color	2 yards each of 1/2 inch wide yellow and blue ribbon
16 eggs (for shaping only)	
1 quantity Royal Icing*	

Makes 8
Preparation time:
1 hour plus making icings and drying time
Freezing:
Not recommended

1. Cut the icing in half and color pale yellow and pale blue.
2. Dust the eggs with cornstarch and place on a rack.
3. Roll out a quarter of the yellow icing on a surface sprinkled with cornstarch and cut out 2 oval shapes large enough to half-cover an egg. Place over 2 eggs and lightly mold to shape. Trim the edge to neaten.
4. Repeat to make 6 more yellow half-shells and 8 blue half egg shells, using the remaining yellow and the blue icing.
5. Roll out the trimmings and cut out flowers, if you wish, using flower cutters. Leave the eggs and flowers to dry overnight in a warm place.
6. Divide the royal icing in half and color yellow and blue. Place in separate waxed paper piping bags fitted with small star tips.
7. Remove the sugar shells from the eggs and pipe a thin line of matching icing around the edges. Fill if you wish, then sandwich matching shells together.
8. Pipe a row of shells around the join. Tie with pretty ribbon or attach the molding icing flowers with a little royal icing. Leave to dry completely, then pack into pretty baskets or boxes.

EASTER DELIGHTS

1-egg quantity Gingerbread Dough*	1 egg white, beaten lightly
2 tablespoons Apricot Glaze*	FINISHING TOUCH:
1 lb ready-to-roll icing green, yellow and lavender food color	1 1/2 yards each of 1/8 inch wide lavender, green and yellow ribbon

1. Make and ice the cookies as for Festive Fancies (page 60), up to end of stage 3.
2. Knead the icing trimmings together and color a quarter green, a quarter lavender and a half yellow.

3. Mold 12 violet leaves, 12 daffodil leaves and 24 stems from the green icing. Mold 12 daffodils, 6 buds, 6 chicks and 36 tiny eggs from the yellow icing; mold 12 violets from the lavender icing and a little yellow icing (see pages 78–79). Leave all the decorations in a warm place to dry.

4. Arrange the violets and leaves on the hearts, securing with egg white, and thread with lavender ribbon.

5. Arrange the daffodils, buds, leaves and stems on the square cookies, securing with egg white, and thread with green or yellow ribbon.

6. Arrange the eggs around the edge of the oval cookies, with the chicks in the center. Secure with egg white and thread with yellow or green ribbon.

7. Leave to dry completely, then wrap in plastic wrap to store.

Makes 18
Preparation time: 1 hour plus making dough and icing, and drying time
Cooking time: 10–15 minutes
Freezing: Not recommended

QUICK MIX CAKE

1 cup self-rising flour　　　*½ cup soft margarine*
1 teaspoon baking powder　*2 eggs*
½ cup superfine sugar

Makes 2-egg quantity
Preparation time: 10 minutes
Cooking time: see individual recipes
Freezing: Not recommended unbaked

1. Sift the flour and baking powder into a bowl. Add the sugar, margarine, eggs and any flavorings (see below).
2. Mix together with a wooden spoon, then beat for 2–3 minutes, until smooth and glossy; alternatively, beat with an electric mixer until just smooth. Use as required.

Where a recipe specifies a 1-egg or 4-egg quantity, simply halve or double the above ingredients. For a 3-egg quantity, use half as much of each ingredient again.

FLAVORINGS
Chocolate. Add 1 tablespoon cocoa powder blended with 1 tablespoon boiling water.
Coffee. Add 2 teaspoons instant coffee blended with 1 teaspoon boiling water.
Citrus. Add 1 teaspoon grated orange, lemon or lime rind.
Peppermint. Add ½ teaspoon each peppermint extract and green food coloring.

BEATEN SPONGE CAKE

2 eggs　　　　　　　　　*½ teaspoon baking*
¼ cup superfine sugar　　*powder*
½ cup all-purpose flour

Makes 2-egg quantity
Preparation time: 10 minutes
Cooking time: see individual recipes
Freezing: Not recommended unbaked

1. Place the eggs and sugar in a heatproof bowl over a saucepan of hot water and beat until thick and pale.
2. Remove the bowl from the heat and continue beating until the beater leaves a thick trail and the mixture is cool.
3. Sift on the flour and baking powder and carefully fold in using a large metal spoon.

Where a recipe specifies a 1-egg or 4-egg quantity, simply halve or double the above ingredients, but do not increase the baking powder. For a 3-egg quantity, use half as much again of each ingredient except the baking powder.

GINGERBREAD DOUGH

2 tablespoons honey
1 tablespoon molasses
2 tablespoons margarine
1 1/2 cups whole wheat
flour

1/2 teaspoon baking soda,
blended with 1 teaspoon
cold water
1–2 teaspoons ground
ginger
1 egg yolk

Makes 1-egg quantity
Preparation time: 10 minutes
Cooking time: see individual recipes
Freezing: Recommended

1. Place the honey, molasses, and margarine in a pan and heat gently, stirring, until melted. Remove from the heat and add the remaining ingredients.
2. Mix to a soft dough, knead on a lightly floured surface until smooth, then use as required.

COOKIE DOUGH

1 1/4 cups all-purpose flour
2 tablespoons cornstarch
1/3 cup margarine
3 tablespoons superfine
sugar

1/2 teaspoon vanilla
1 egg white
2 tablespoons milk

Makes 1 quantity
Preparation time: 10 minutes
Cooking time: see individual recipes
Freezing: Recommended

1. Sift the flour and cornstarch into a bowl and rub in the margarine until the mixture resembles breadcrumbs.
2. Stir in remaining ingredients and mix to a firm dough. Knead on a lightly floured surface until smooth, then use as required.

BREAD DOUGH

2 cups sifted all-purpose
flour
1/2 teaspoon superfine
sugar
1/2 teaspoon salt

1 tablespoon butter
1 teaspoon easy-blend
dried yeast
about 1/2 cup warm water

Makes 1 quantity
Preparation time: 20–25 minutes
Cooking time: see individual recipes
Freezing: Not recommended unbaked

1. Place the flour, sugar and salt in a bowl and rub in the butter until the mixture resembles breadcrumbs.
2. Stir in the yeast and enough water to mix to a soft dough. Knead on a lightly floured surface for about 5 minutes, until smooth and no longer sticky. Return to the bowl, cover with plastic wrap and leave in a warm place for 5–10 minutes. Use as required.

BUTTER ICING

½ cup butter, softened   *1 teaspoon lemon juice*
2 cups sifted powdered
*   sugar*

Makes 1
quantity/½ lb
Preparation time:
5 minutes
Freezing:
Recommended

1. Beat the butter in a bowl until light and fluffy.
2. Beat in the powdered sugar a little at a time.
3. Beat in the lemon juice and any flavoring (see p. 74). Use as required.

ROYAL ICING

1 egg white   *food color (optional)*
2 cups sifted powdered
*   sugar*

Makes 1
quantity/½ lb
Preparation time:
5 minutes
Freezing:
Not recommended

1. Place the egg white in a clean bowl. Add sufficient powdered sugar to form the consistency of unwhipped cream, mixing well with a wooden spoon.
2. Continue adding powdered sugar until the desired consistency has been reached and the icing is smooth and glossy. Add any food color.
3. Cover the surface with damp plastic wrap and set aside. Stir before use to disperse air bubbles. Keep bowl covered while applying icing.

GLACÉ ICING

Thick glacé icing comes in very handy for attaching candy, balls or any small details to a dry molding icing or marzipan surface.

Makes 2–3
tablespoons
Preparation time:
5 minutes
Freezing:
Not recommended

½ cup powdered sugar   *1 teaspoon warm water*
                                *   (approximately)*

Sift the powdered sugar into a small bowl. Gradually add enough water to form a thick icing, which peaks when a spoon is drawn from it. Use immediately.

APRICOT GLAZE

It's a good idea to make a large quantity, as it will keep in a screw-top jar in the refrigerator for up to 2 months.

1 lb apricot jam   *3 tablespoons water*

1. Place the jam and water in a saucepan, heat gently until melted, then boil rapidly for 30 seconds.
2. Strain, rubbing through as much of the fruit as possible. Pour into a clean jar, seal and store in the refrigerator. Use as required.

Makes 1 lb glaze
Preparation time:
5 minutes
Freezing:
Not recommended

QUICK MOLDING ICING

This easy-to-make icing is suitable for icing cakes and for making decorations. It will keep for up to 3 months.

1 egg white   *4 cups sifted powdered*
2 tablespoons liquid   *sugar*
*   glucose*

1. Place the egg white and glucose in a bowl. Add the powdered sugar and mix together with a wooden spoon.
2. Knead with the fingers until the mixture forms a ball, then knead on a surface dusted with powdered sugar until smooth and free from cracks.
3. Wrap in plastic wrap or in a plastic bag until required.

Makes 1
quantity/1¼ lb
Preparation time:
5 minutes
Freezing:
Not recommended

NOTE: To apply molding icing, roll out to a ¼ inch thickness, lay the icing over the cake and gently smooth with hands dusted with cornstarch to the shape of the cake. Trim excess icing away at the base or join and rub the icing surface in circular movements until smooth and glossy. For best results, leave the iced cake in a warm, dry place for a few hours or overnight to dry.

MOLDED AND CUT-OUT NOVELTY DECORATIONS

Novelty decorations can be molded or cut very simply from ready-to-roll icing or molding icing (above); some may be made from ready-made marzipan.

Food color may be kneaded evenly into the icing or marzipan or applied with a fine paintbrush to the finished decoration.

For best results, the finished decorations should be set aside in a warm dry place for a few hours or overnight before applying to the cake.

Necklace: Roll out white molding icing to a ¼ inch thickness. Using tiny cutters, cut out various shapes. Apply colored blossom tints with a fine paintbrush to make the surface glitter. Thread onto liquorice, fine pasta or thread to make a necklace, bracelet or pendants.

Rings and earrings: Cut out small circles of molding icing to make rings, press colored balls and candies in position for 'gems'. Cut out molding icing shapes and stud with 'gems' for earrings. Leave to set.

Holly leaves: Roll out green marzipan or molding icing thinly on a surface dusted with cornstarch. Cut out leaf shapes, using holly leaf cutters or a cardboard cut-out as a guide. Mark on veins with a knife and place over pieces of dowel stick sprinkled with cornstarch to dry.

Bucket: Mold red molding icing into a flat-ended cone shape. Using the end of a fine paintbrush, press to hollow out the inside to form a bucket shape. Mold a handle and press in position.

Cuckoo: Shape a small ball of brown marzipan into a body with a pointed head. Shape 2 tiny wings and press onto the sides of the body. Mark eyes and a beak with the pointed end of a fine paintbrush.

Clogs: Shape 2 small balls of red molding icing into clog shapes. Using the end of a fine paintbrush, press to hollow out the inside of each clog.

Grain sacks: Shape 2 or 3 pieces of brown icing into ½ inch thick rectangles measuring 1 inch × ¾ inch. Using the end of a fine paintbrush, hollow out the inside of each to make a sack. Mark the outside with a knife. Fill each with sunflower or sesame seeds if you wish.

Molded flowers: Roll different-colored pieces of molding icing into small balls, press into petal shapes and curl edges into the center. Press 3 colored petals together, trim off stems and leave to set.

Christmas roses: Roll 7 tiny pieces of white molding icing into balls. Using hands, dusted with cornstarch, press 5 into petal shapes. Flatten another ball into a circle and arrange the petals, overlapping, on top; sit the flower in a cup-shaped piece of foil. Press remaining ball into the center and stud with stamens made from yellow molding icing. Leave to set in the foil, then remove carefully.

Violets: Roll 5 tiny pieces of violet molding icing into balls; using hands dusted with cornstarch, press into 5 petal shapes. Arrange all the petals together and secure with a little egg white. Press some stamens made with yellow molding icing in the center. To make buds, arrange and secure 3 petal shapes together. To make stems, roll pieces of green molding icing with the fingertips into thin rolls, tapering at the ends. To make leaves, press out balls of green molding icing into leaf shapes. Mark on veins with a knife.

Daffodils: Take 7 tiny balls of yellow molding icing. Press 6 into petal shapes. Add more yellow food coloring to the remaining ball and, using the end of a fine paintbrush, press out to make the trumpet shape. Assemble the petals and trumpet center, using a little egg white. To make buds, take 5 balls of icing, shape 4 petals; make the trumpet shape as above. Press the petals onto the cone. To make stems, roll pieces of green molding icing with the fingertips into thin stems, tapering at the ends. Flatten with the fingers to make leaves.

Easter chicks: Shape a small ball of yellow molding icing into a head with a beak and a larger ball into a body. Press out a tiny wing shape and assemble the chick using egg white. Mark eyes and beak with the end of a fine paintbrush.

Illustrated above: Molded flower; Christmas rose; Violet (showing stems, leaves and bud); Daffodil (showing stems, leaves and bud); Easter chick.

INDEX

Photography by: James Jackson
Designed by: Sue Storey
Home economist: Janice Murfitt
Stylist: Sue Russell
Color Illustration by: Linda Smith
Line drawings by: Holderness & Long
U.S. Consultant Editor: Carla Capalbo